BLUE BANNER
BIOGRAPHY

Le'Veon
BELL

John Bankston

Mitchell Lane

PUBLISHERS
2001 SW 31st Avenue
Hallandale, FL 33009
www.mitchelllane.com

Mitchell Lane
PUBLISHERS

Printing   1   2   3   4   5   6   7   8   9

Blue Banner Biographies

Library of Congress Cataloging-in-Publication Data
Names: Bankston, John, 1974- author.
Title: Le'Veon Bell / by John Bankston.
Description: Hallandale, FL : Mitchell Lane Publishers, [2019] | Series: Blue banner biographies | Includes bibliographical references and index.
Identifiers: LCCN 2018007999 | ISBN 9781680201802 (library bound)
Subjects: LCSH: Bell, Le'veon, — Juvenile literature. | Football players — United States — Biography — Juvenile literature.
Classification: LCC GV939 .B4553 2018 | DDC 796.33092 [B] — dc23
LC record available at https://lccn.loc.gov/2018007999

ABOUT THE AUTHOR: Born in Boston, Massachusetts, John Bankston began writing professionally while still a teenager. Since then, more than 200 of his articles have been published in magazines and newspapers across the country. He is the author of more than 100 nonfiction books for children and young adults, including Mitchell Lane biographies of Abby Wambach, Kevin Durant, and Selena Gomez. Today he lives in coastal Florida.

Blue Banner Biography

Le'Veon Bell runs onto the field before his Pittsburgh Steelers host the Jacksonville Jaguars in a National Football League (NFL) playoff game on January 14, 2018. The underdog Jaguars upset the Steelers, 45–42.

Taking the Lead

1

Le'Veon Bell needed to do something. It was 2009, and his Groveport (Ohio) Madison High School football team was losing. At halftime, he joined the rest of the Cruisers team in the locker room.

The players waited. Some of them expected the coach to give a pep talk. Or maybe the quarterback. Quarterbacks usually provide leadership for their teams.

Le'Veon was a running back. Cruiser fans knew him because he scored so often. But running backs rarely give pep talks.

It didn't matter. Le'Veon had something to say. He made a short speech. Then he repeated something the school principal, Donis Toler, Jr. often said. "It's hard but it's fair."

Toler was nearby. He was stunned. Le'Veon was using the same motto Toler's father, a football coach, frequently used. Now Le'Veon was using it to inspire his teammates.

"It's about sacrifice," Toler told the website mlive. com. "It means that if you work hard that when it's all said and done at the end of the day, it will be fair."

The Cruisers went on to win the game. Le'Veon's speech didn't just help his team. It helped him too.

Watching the young man, Toler realized that he had become a leader. He was ready to join a top college team. Unfortunately, none of them had asked Le'Veon to play for them.

Every fall, coaches and scouts for the country's best college football teams visit high schools across the country. They go to games, watching players from the stands. They watch videos of games. They read stories about games and pay attention to how a player is ranked.

As a junior, Le'Veon had been recruited by several lower-ranked colleges.

As a junior, Le'Veon had been recruited by several lower-ranked colleges. Their teams did not win championships. Few of their players turned pro.

On the football field, Le'Veon was patient. He usually didn't run as soon as he had the ball. He waited. He watched his blockers. He looked for openings. On video he didn't look patient. He looked slow.

Long before he was a principal, Toler was also a running back. Soon after Le'Veon's speech, Toler spoke to his old coach, Mark Dantonio. He was the head football coach at Michigan State University. Toler told him that Le'Veon had what it took to play for the Spartans. Dantonio asked assistant coach Dan Enos to go see Le'Veon play.

Michigan State coach Mark Dantonio and Le'Veon Bell walk to the stadium before an NCAA college football game in September, 2015.

There was one problem. Football season was over.

When Enos arrived at Groveport Madison, Le'Veon wasn't racing across a football field. He was running on a basketball court. Enos didn't even watch the game. "I made it through warmups," Enos told mlive.com. As soon as they ended, he called Dantonio. "Man, this guy can play," he said. "We've got to take him."

It was a life-changing opportunity. It was also one Le'Veon Bell might never have gotten. He has often said that he owes his success to the hard work of his mother.

Dreams and Discipline

When Lisa Bell gave birth to her first child in Reynoldsburg, Ohio, on February 18, 1992, she wanted him to stand out. She knew his first name should start with an 'L,' like hers. "I was just playing letters, and I came up with Le'Veon," she told *The Washington Post* in 2017. "I knew for sure I didn't want anything that was common." As he spent his childhood in nearby Columbus, the Ohio state capital, people who met him quickly realized he was anything but common.

Le'Veon was not an only child for long. His brother, Lavonte, was born in 1995, while Clarence followed in 1999. Their father was often gone. By the time Clarence was born, he was no longer around. Life for the Bells became very hard.

"There's times when they were eating," Lisa Bell admitted on E-60. "I was hungry and I didn't eat." She worked at several different jobs. For a while, she was a secretary for the Columbus school district. At night, she worked at a local mall as a security guard. She was also a teaching assistant. But no matter how hard she worked, there was never enough money.

There also wasn't much time to spend with her family. As Le'Veon got older, he told her he didn't like how hard she had to work. Lisa Bell said hard work was a part of life. "My mom did a great job of not displaying her struggle," Le'Veon told E-60. "She was always happy."

Fortunately, Lisa Bell was not alone. Her parents lived next door. Her older brother, Clarence, was close by. He helped as much as he could. When Le'Veon was only four, his uncle introduced him to football.

"At the time, I think I just loved running from people because it was like tag to me," he told E-60. His older cousin played pee-wee football. When Le'Veon turned five, he joined the Linden Lumber Patriots. By the time he was in elementary school, it was about more than playing tag. It was also about learning.

Uncle Clarence made sure he learned from the best. The two of them watched professional and college football games together. Clarence pointed out the good and bad choices that players made. "We had a conversation," Clarence told *The Washington Post*. "Where the play is going, that hole might not be there. You can't just take the ball and blast up in there. You may want to wait."

Lisa Bell knew her son was talented. He told her that when he played in the National Football League (NFL), he'd make sure she didn't have to work. She replied, "If you play in the NFL, you're gonna play for the [Pittsburgh] Steelers."

Le'Veon was often bigger than other kids his age. In some games, he was younger than the others. He was still

Le'Veon's mother wanted him to be a Pittsburgh Steeler. Her wish came true. Here he takes part in a practice in London, England in 2013, two days before his first game.

> *Le'Veon was often bigger than other kids his age.*

one of the best. For all of sixth grade, he avoided being tackled. Finally, during the championship game, he was brought down. He admitted on SB Nation that "I was disappointed." When he asked his mother if she was upset with him, she told him getting tackled was part of the game.

Before Le'Veon entered middle school, his mother made a huge sacrifice. He told SB Nation that his Columbus neighborhood was "rugged." It was a place with crime and drug dealing. His mother decided they should move. "I don't know if I would be where I am now if I had stayed," he added.

With less than 6,000 people, Groveport was one of the smaller suburbs of Columbus. It was certainly a big change from the big city. For Lisa Bell, moving meant that her work was further away than it had been. For Le'Veon, it meant his talents stood out more than they would have in a larger program. He did well at Groveport Madison Middle School. And he excelled when he got to high school. Toler was a big reason for that. He worked hard to help Le'Veon succeed both on and off the football field. He became a mentor.

As Le'Veon later explained on "Le'Veon Bell: A Running Backstory," Toler told him right away, "'You're not the man here. I'm the man here.' My mom would always come at me, but I didn't really have like a father figure to say 'don't do this, don't do that.' He kind of took that over."

When Toler first saw Le'Veon practice, he was worried. Le'Veon seemed to be taking too long to run the ball. It was only when Toler saw him play in a game that the principal realized something. Like his name, Le'Veon was special. He didn't hurry. He didn't race. He waited.

Waiting allowed him to find openings in the line of scrimmage. These were places where he could cut around defenders. "He just knew he had to be patient," Toler told *The Washington Post*, "because he knew the other way wasn't going to work."

Although Le'Veon loved football, it wasn't his only sport. He played on the school's basketball team and ran track. Both sports improved his speed. Basketball also helped his footwork. During his junior year as a basketball player, he earned second-team All-OCC Division honors. As a track and field athlete, he competed in both the 100- and 200-meter dashes. His best event was the high jump, where he cleared 6'8". That made him one of the top high jumpers in Ohio.

Yet it was on the football field that Le'Veon really stood out. Every year his rushing yardage improved. In his senior year, he rushed for 1,333 yards on 200 carries. He scored 21 touchdowns. Le'Veon also earned All-Ohio Capital Conference Ohio Division first-team honors.

For his coaches, one game stood out. It was the first game of the season during his senior year. The Cruisers needed a score to win. The opposing team had just punted. Le'Veon caught the ball.

"And he just stands there. And he doesn't move," assistant coach Bryan Schoonover recalled on SB Nation. "And we are screaming, 'Run! You run!' And his buddy comes down and makes a block and [Le'Veon] goes up the sideline. [He] plants his foot in the ground, cuts completely across the field in front of their entire team. Walks in the end zone and flips the ball to the official. It's the best high school play I've ever seen in my life." Afterward he asked Le'Veon how he knew to make the play. He replied, "I don't know, I just saw it."

By then Le'Veon was considering playing college football for schools like Eastern Michigan, Bowling Green, and Marshall. "Watching Bell as a junior in

> **Le'Veon was able to enroll at Michigan State and participate in the Spartans' spring practice.**

camp, he was kind of just a guy. He was a big back, but he wasn't overly explosive," recruiting analyst Josh Helmholdt told *USA Today* in 2012. "He was a dime a dozen." One recruiting service ranked him number 211 among all high school running backs in the country.

Toler believes he knows why. "Things came to him so easy that he just didn't feel like he had to work that hard," he told SB Nation. "Which he didn't have to." When Le'Veon realized the top programs weren't looking at him, he knew he had to change. He was inspired by his mom. He tried to work as hard as she did. The summer before his senior year, he trained and practiced. He worked harder than he ever had.

Luck was on Le'Veon's side. Several running backs whom Michigan State had recruited were unable to attend. The school offered him a scholarship. Toler had urged him to take online courses so he could graduate early from high school. As a result, Le'Veon was able to enroll at Michigan State and participate in the Spartans' spring practice. Playing there meant being one step closer to his NFL dream.

On the
Spartan Field

College can be difficult. For many students, living away from home is hard. So is leaving family and friends. It can be even harder for athletes. Most college players were the best in their high schools. Many of them fail to make a mark at the next level. Freshmen often spend their first season on the bench. For Le'Veon, it was different. The coaches took a chance on him and decided to let him play right away. It paid off.

Division I football is the highest level of college competition in the United States. Michigan State belongs to the Big Ten Conference, the oldest conference in the country. Member schools are large and hard to get into. Many have won national championships in football. So when Le'Veon took to the field, it was a big deal.

On September 4, 2010 Le'Veon played in the season's first game. The Spartans took on Western Michigan. He carried the ball ten times, rushing for 141 yards. No freshman in school history had carried for 100 yards in his first game. He also scored two touchdowns. Le'Veon was named the Big Ten Freshman of the Week. There would be more awards and honors.

During his first year, he was on the field for all of the team's 13 games. He rushed for 605 yards. He

Le'Veon smiles as he leaves the field after his first college game. He rushed for a freshman-record 141 yards as Michigan State defeated Western Michigan 38–14.

> **By the time he was a junior, Le'Veon was a fan favorite.**

scored eight touchdowns. The next year, he racked up 948 rushing yards and scored 13 touchdowns. By the time he was a junior, Le'Veon was a fan favorite. He led the Big Ten Conference in rushing attempts (382) that season and finished second in rushing yards with 1,793. He received All-Big Ten first-team honors.

Lisa Bell was there for much of it. She helped Le'Veon deal with being away from his family by attending every MSU home game. He wrote about his mother on The Caldron. He called the article, "My Vote for MVP [Most

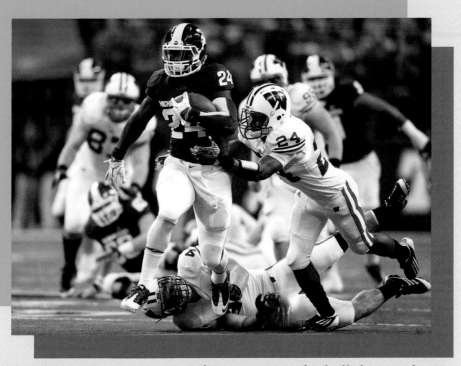

During his sophomore year, Le'Veon carries the ball during the Big Ten Conference Championship game against the Wisconsin Badgers. Wisconsin defeated the Spartans, 42–39.

Valuable Player]." "When I was at Michigan State, she traveled to our bowl game against [Texas Christian University] and cooked in the hotel's kitchen; she actually brought her own roasters and crockpots because the hotel didn't have an oven," he wrote. "She's always had everything covered . . . my mother was the first one to show me how valuable a tight game plan really is."

Le'Veon holds up the trophy for offensive player of the game after the Buffalo Wild Wings Bowl against the TCU Horned Frogs in December, 2012.

Le'Veon enjoyed playing for MSU. Yet every game was a risk. If he got injured, he might never play in the NFL. If that happened, he'd never make any money as a football player. His childhood dreams of helping his mom would die.

In 2013, after his junior year had ended, Le'Veon announced that he would enter the NFL Draft that spring. That is where pro football teams choose the best college players. Before he entered the draft, he made a pinky swear to his mother. He promised he would go back to college later and earn his degree.

"The biggest reason for me coming out is that I'm ready," he told *USA Today*. "This has been my goal since I was 5 or 6 years old. I actually have a chance to go and get that opportunity."

Pro football teams watched Le'Veon play at the NFL Scouting Combine. They liked what they saw. He stood 6-foot-1 and weighed a solid 225 pounds. The Pittsburgh Steelers picked him in the second round of the draft. For Lisa Bell, it was an early Mother's Day present.

"She grew up a Steelers fan, everyone in my family did," Le'Veon said on Steelers.com. "My grandpa grew up a fan of the team. That is where she got it from. He was in tears when they drafted me. . . . I am happy to be here. I am glad it's not too far away. My mom can drive to the games."

Le'Veon in action during the NFL Combine in February, 2013.

Despite leaving before his senior year, Le'Veon ranked number seven in MSU history for both rushing yards and rushing touchdowns. Many who had watched him play thought he was the best college running back in the country. They wondered if he'd be the best pro running back as well.

4

Starting His Career

During the summer of 2013, Le'Veon got ready. He trained hard for his first pro football game. Instead, it seemed at first that he might not play at all. Before the season began, he hurt his knee. Then, while playing a preseason game against Washington, he sprained his foot. For a running back, it could be a crippling injury.

Fortunately, Le'Veon didn't take long to recover. He only missed the team's first three games. That meant that his first pro game wasn't in the U.S. It was in England. Each year, several NFL teams travel to London to play there. In Europe, when people say "football," they usually mean "soccer." On September 29th, Le'Veon took the field and showed local fans how American football is played. He made two rushing touchdowns. By the end of his first season as a Steeler, he had broken Steeler legend Franco Harris's record for total yards—rushing and receiving—by a rookie running back. He had amassed a total of 1,259 yards.

In 2014, Le'Veon prepared for his second season. But on August 20th, he and his teammate LeGarrette Blount were pulled over by police. They discovered drugs in the car. Le'Veon entered a program for first-

Le'Veon dives into the end zone during the NFL International Series game between the Pittsburgh Steelers and the Minnesota Vikings on September 29, 2013.

time offenders. If he stayed out of trouble, his record would remain clean.

That year, he was ranked second in the NFL for both rushing yards and total yards from scrimmage. He earned All-Pro and Pro Bowl honors. He believed that 2015, his third year with the Steelers, would be even better. He hoped to take the team into the playoffs. He began playing in the team's third game.

On September 29th, Le'Veon took the field and showed local fans how American football is played.

He rushed for 556 yards in the next six games. Even with the lost games, he was ready to once again reach the top of the NFL rankings.

That changed on November 1. During a game against the Cincinnati Bengals, he was racing toward the sidelines. Bengals linebacker Vontaze Burfict tackled Le'Veon. His right leg was trapped beneath the bigger man's body and bent backward. Le'Veon was carted off the field.

Le'Veon being grabbed by Vontaze Burfict during the Cincinnati Bengals and Pittsburgh Steelers game on November 1, 2015.

5 Playoffs

The injury ended his season. He needed surgery and time to heal. Despite the setback, Le'Veon remained hopeful. He believed that 2016 would be the year that he would help take his team to the playoffs. The Steelers were a force that season. When they beat the Washington Redskins in the first game, fans felt certain that this was their year. Although they'd reached the playoffs the previous two years, they had been knocked out before reaching the AFC (American Football Conference) Championship Game. The winner of that game advances to the Super Bowl. That goal got closer when Le'Veon rejoined his teammates on October 2, against the Kansas City Chiefs. His 144 yards on 18 carries helped the Steelers win easily, 43–14.

The Steelers finished the season 11-5 and finished first in the AFC North Division. They made the playoffs.

On January 8, 2017 Le'Veon played in the AFC Wild Card game. It was his first NFL post-season game. He set a Steelers' playoff record with 167 yards rushing. He helped them defeat the Miami Dolphins, 30-12.

Going into the Divisional Round, many people saw Le'Veon as the reason his team would win or lose. "He's not the fastest guy, not the biggest guy, but he's

Le'Veon is tackled just short of the goal line during the Wild Card playoff game against the Miami Dolphins in January, 2017.

probably the smartest runner in the NFL," his Michigan State teammate and fellow running back Larry Caper explained to *The Washington Post* in 2017.

In that game, he broke his own record by rushing for 170 yards as the Steelers won a narrow victory over the Kansas City Chiefs, 18-16.

> *The final hurdle to the Super Bowl was the AFC Championship Game.*

The final hurdle to the Super Bowl was the AFC Championship Game. Unfortunately, the New England Patriots soundly defeated the Steelers, 36–17. Pittsburgh could take some small comfort when the Patriots went on to win the Super Bowl.

Le'Veon focused on other interests. He donated $750,000 to his high school so they could fix their football field. He set up an organization to help high school athletes at Groveport. And he ran a summer football camp at the nearby middle school. Using the name Juice, he also released a hip-hop album, *Post Interview*. Most important, he became a father, welcoming his daughter Melodie.

Le'Veon Bell (right) goes up against Hall of Fame running back Marshall Faulk during ABC's Celebrity Family Feud. Players from the National Football League Players Association (NFLPA) spar off against each other to win money for a charity of their choice. The show aired on July 9, 2017.

In July 2017, he did not show up for training camp. The team's general manager, Kevin Colbert, was unhappy. "My feeling is there's nothing to be gained by a holdout," he told the *Pittsburgh Post-Gazette*. It hurts him because he's not working with his teammates."

Eventually he joined the Steelers. He had a great season. He rushed for 1,291 yards and scored nine touchdowns. He caught 85 passes. Two of them went for touchdowns. Pittsburgh also had a great season. The team won 13 games while losing just three. But their season

Le'Veon catches a pass in front of Telvin Smith of the Jacksonville Jaguars for a 19-yard touchdown reception in the third quarter during the AFC Divisional Playoff game on January 14, 2018.

Le'Veon runs into the NFC defense during the NFL Pro Bowl game between the AFC and the NFC on January 28, 2018 at Camping World Stadium in Orlando, Florida. The AFC defeated the NFC 24 to 23.

ended in the Divisional Round of the playoffs. The Jacksonville Jaguars upset the favored Steelers, 45–42. The Super Bowl would have to wait at least another year.

When the Steelers first signed him, Le'Veon told a reporter at the *Charlestown Gazette*, "I've been competing from day one, just make those other guys better, make the other running backs better, and at the same time they're going to make me better. I'm going to help this team the best that I can and get a Super Bowl." Pittsburgh fans hope that he will be able to keep that promise in the very near future.

1992   Le'Veon Andrew Bell is born on February 18th in Reynoldsburg, Ohio.

1995   Brother Lavonte is born.

1997   Begins playing peewee football

1999   Brother Clarence is born.

2008   Plays football at Groveport Madison High School.

2010   Begins playing for Michigan State University.

2013   Enters the NFL Draft and is picked in the second round by the Pittsburgh Steelers.

2014   Is named to the NFL All-Pro First Team and Pro Bowl.

2015   Suffers season-ending knee injury.

2016   Helps the Steelers to 11–5 record and AFC North championship.

2017   His daughter Melodie is born.

2018   Competes in the NFL playoffs for the first time.

CAREER STATS

YEAR	TEAM	ATTS	YDS	AVG	TDS
2010	Michigan State	107	605	5.7	8
2011	Michigan State	182	948	5.2	13
2012	Michigan State	382	1,793	4.7	12
2013	Pittsburgh Steelers	244	860	3.5	8
2014	Pittsburgh Steelers	290	1,361	4.7	8
2015	Pittsburgh Steelers	113	556	4.9	3
2016	Pittsburgh Steelers	261	1,268	4.9	7
2017	Pittsburgh Steelers	321	1,291	4.0	9

ATTS = attempts; YDS = yards gained; AVG = average per carry; TDs = touchdowns

Books

Editors of Sports Illustrated Kids. *Football: Then to WOW!* New York: Sports Illustrated, 2014.

Gramling, Gary. *The Football Fanbook: Everything You Need to Become a Gridiron Know-it-All*. New York: Sports Illustrated: 2017.

Hall, Darla. *Go Steelers Activity Book*. In the Sports Zone: 2014.

On the Internet

Le'Veon Bell. https://www.leveonbellrb.com/pages/bio

Le'Veon Bell. Groveport Madison Stats. http://247sports.com/Player/LeVeon-Bell-8205?PlayerInstitution=13122

Le'Veon Bell. Pro Football Reference. http://www.pro-football-reference.com/players/B/BellLe00.htm

Michigan State University Spartans Football. http://www.msuspartans.com/sports/m-footbl/msu-m-footbl-body.html

Periodicals

Bell, Jarrett. "Early entrants wrestle with choices." *USA Today*, April 15, 2013.

Bouchette, Ed. "Le'Veon Bell is Hurting Himself." *Pittsburgh Post Gazette*, August 9, 2017. http://www.post-gazette.com/sports/steelers/2017/08/09/leveon-bell-contract-status-pittsburgh-steelers-training-camp-holdout/stories/201708090130

Graves, Will. "Le'Veon Bell Plans for the Steelers." *Charleston [WV] Gazette*, July 31, 2013.

Kilgore, Adam. "Steelers' Le'Veon Bell Finds Success on the Ground by Not Rushing." *The Washington Post*, January 12, 2017. https://www.washingtonpost.com/sports/redskins/steelers-leveon-bell-finds-success-on-the-ground-by-not-rushing/2017/01/12/67b4fd24-d8ce-11e6-9a36-1d296534b31e_story.html?utm_term=.1a20980e0534

Oller, Rob. "Le'Veon Bell of Steelers Turning into Man Mom Envisioned." *The Columbus Dispatch*, May 27, 2017. http://www.dispatch.com/sports/20170527/rob-oller--leveon-bell-of-steelers-turning-into-man-mom-envisioned

"Reports RB Le'Veon Bell Lost for Season with Torn MCL." *Sports Illustrated*, November 1, 2015. https://www.si.com/nfl/2015/11/01/piitsburgh-steelers-leveon-bell-leg-injury-update-video

Rexrode, Joe. "Michigan State's Le'Veon Bell Slipped Through Cracks." *USA Today*, September 28, 2012. https://www.usatoday.com/story/sports/ncaaf/2012/09/28/michigan-state-leveon-bell-recruiting/1600735/

Warnemuende, Jeremy. "Bell Named Big Ten Co-Freshman of the Week." *The State News*, September 6, 2010. http://statenews.com/article/2010/09/bell_named_big_ten_cofreshman_of_the_week

Web Sites
Bell, Clarence. https://www.instagram.com/clarencebell01/?hl=en

Bell, LaVonte. https://www.instagram.com/p/yGZz2eyBIs/?hl=en&taken-by=lavontebell

Bell, Le'Veon. "My Vote for MVP." The Caldron. November 27, 2014. https://the-cauldron.com/my-vote-for-mvp-d081cba5fa0e

Cyphers, Steve. "Le'Veon Bell: A Running Backstory." steelers. com, December 12, 2014. http://www.steelers.com/video-and-audio/videos/LeVeon-Bell-A-running-backstory/7c56a02a-8276-4762-8dd4-563b51505a5d

"E-60: A Mother's Dedication." http://www.espn.com/espnw/video/13872303/e60-mother-dedication

Leung, Diamond. "Michigan State Coach Mark Dantonio's Recruitment of Le'Veon Bell Defined by Generations-old Saying, 'It's hard, but it's fair.'" mlive.com, September 13, 2012. http://www.mlive.com/spartans/index.ssf/2012/09/michigan_states_recruitment_of.html

Rollett, Rebecca. "Character (Ac)Counts: RB Le'Veon Bell." behindthesteelcurtain.com, December 12, 2014. https://www.behindthesteelcurtain.com/pittsburgh-steelers-nfl-features-news-blog-long-form/2014/12/12/7383007/character-ac-counts-rb-leveon-bell

Varley, Teresa. "An Early Mother's Day Gift for Bell's Mom." steelers.com, May 9, 2013. http://www.steelers.com/news/article-1/An-early-Mothers-Day-gift-for-Bells-mom/93160ca8-51f2-484d-9684-2a5300442a28

Videos

"Le'Veon Bell Went from Unwanted to Unstoppable." SB Nation, November 3, 2015. https://www.sbnation.com/nfl/2015/11/3/9664050/leveon-bell-video-interview-profile